SkillAbilities
FOR YOUTH MINISTRY

Setting Boundaries With Youth

How to Discipline With Understanding

by Kathleen M. Sorensen

ABINGDON PRESS

Nashville, Tennessee

About the Writer
Kathleen Sorensen serves as assistant director of the Boys Town Center for Adolescent and Family Spirituality. During the past ten years, she has been with Boys Town, where she contributes extensively to the development and implementation of Boys Town's skills-based religious education curriculum.

Acknowledgments
Thanks to Father Val Peter, Executive Director, and Tom Everson, Director of Religious Education, Father Flanagan's Boys' Home, Boys Town, Nebraska; Pastor Jeff Huber, Calvary United Methodist Church, Colorado Springs, Colorado.

SKILLABILITIES FOR YOUTH WORKERS
Setting Boundaries With Youth:
How to Discipline With Understanding
Volume 11

SKILLABILITIES FOR YOUTH WORKERS, Vol.11
Copyright © 1998 by Abingdon Press. All rights reserved. No part of this work may be reproduced or transmitted in any form or by any means, electronic or mechanical, including photocopying or recording, or by any information storage or retrieval system, except as may be expressly permitted by the 1976 Copyright Act or in writing by the publisher. For some material, permission to photocopy is on the page. Requests for permission should be addressed to Abingdon Press, P.O. Box 801, 201 Eighth Avenue South, Nashville, TN 37202-0801.Printed in the United States of America.

Scripture quotations in this publication, unless otherwise indicated, are from the New Revised Standard Version Bible, copyright © 1989 by the Division of Christian Education of the National Council of Churches of Christ in the United States of America. Used by permission.

ISBN 0-687-08780-5

98 99 00 01 02 03 04 05 06—10 9 8 7 6 5 4 3 2 1

EDITORIAL AND DESIGN TEAM	**ADMINISTRATIVE TEAM**
Editor: Crystal A. Zinkiewicz	**Publisher:** Neil M. Alexander
Production Editor: Sheila K. Hewitt	**Vice President:** Harriett Jane Olson
Design Manager: Phillip D. Francis	**Executive Editor, Teaching and Study Resources:** Duane A. Ewers
Designer: Sheila K. Hewitt	**Editor of Youth Resources:** M. Steven Games
Cover Design: Diana Maio & Phillip D. Francis	

CONTENTS

	page
WHY DO THIS? What boundaries are and how they benefit youth and youth ministry	4
WHAT'S THE WORD? What the Bible says about boundaries	16
SETTING BOUNDARIES—CREATING COVENANT Building a firm foundation	25
MAINTAINING BOUNDARIES 2 tried-and-true tactics	38
WHEN A BOUNDARY IS BROKEN Consequences and grace	43
BASIC BOUNDARIES 10 boundaries for discussions everyone can feel good about	58
BOUNDARIES FOR ONE-TO-ONES 3 crucial things to keep in mind for youth-adult interactions	60
PREVENTING PROBLEMS Boundary-setting skills for youth	63
MINI-WORKSHOP Leadership training	67
THE BIG PICTURE How does this SkillAbility fit in? What's next? Who's there to help?	71

WHY DO THIS?

A **boundary** is a limit and a standard.

A boundary tells us
what is acceptable behavior—
**what to do,
what not to do.**

Some Examples of Boundaries

Why Do This?

Boundaries Are Assets!

Search Institute has identified 40 external and internal assets that pay off by helping young people become emotionally healthy and and socially competent adults. Among them are six specifically categorized as "Boundaries and Expectations." Although not stated in terms of youth ministry, they also apply there:

FAMILY BOUNDARIES   **Asset #11**
Family has clear rules and consequences and monitors whereabouts.

SCHOOL BOUNDARIES   **Asset #12**
School provides clear rules and consequences.

NEIGHBORHOOD BOUNDARIES   **Asset #13**
Neighbors would report undesirable behavior to family.

ADULT ROLE MODELS   **Asset #14**
Parent(s) and other adults model responsible behavior.

POSITIVE PEER INFLUENCE   **Asset #15**
Young person's best friends model responsible behavior.

HIGH EXPECTATIONS   **Asset #16**
Both parents and teachers press young person to achieve.

© 1996 Search Institute, 700 South 3rd Street, Minneapolis, MN 55415, 612-376-8955. Used by permission.

Setting Boundaries With Youth

We **all** need to know the limits and the expectations.

Knowing the boundaries is freeing. What's inside the limits is safe.

Why Do This?

Emotional boundaries enable us to protect personal thoughts, feelings, and experiences.

Churches undertake the awesome task of helping youth grow spiritually. One way is to create and maintain a welcoming atmosphere. Sprucing up your meeting space can help, but it's more effective to set and maintain specific boundaries and expectations for how to treat one another.

Setting Boundaries With Youth

Spiritual growth is based on building good relationships with God and others through sharing faith, going deep into heart-matters, asking questions, praying, and so forth. Each of these involve risking and trusting.

Our task is to create and maintain an environment with clear emotional boundaries so that youth can be assured that they will be

respected,

listened to,

and cared for—

no matter what!

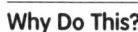

Why Do This?

Physical boundaries enable us to protect and honor our bodies as the "temple of the Holy Spirit."
—1 Corinthians 6:19

As adults, we need to create and maintain a safe environment for youth. Whether in a classroom or on a ski trip, a community service project, retreat, or some other event, youth need clear and specific instructions and rules.

"While on the scavenger hunt, remain in groups of four."

"Ask permission from your retreat leader before leaving the building."

"We will solve conflicts through discussion."

"Youth do not ride in cars driven by other youth unless they provide written permission from parents."

Benefits for Youth

External rules
>   can become
>>   internal guides.

Established and enforced boundaries help youth recognize the limits and enable them to take personal responsibility for their actions. Then...

Discipline
>   becomes
>>   self-discipline.

Boundaries help youth learn how to **respect** and **relate to others;** and in doing so, they feel better about themselves.

Boundaries help create an environment where youth can feel safe and comfortable enough **to open themselves** more **to God's love** and grace.

Why Do This?

When what is expected and appropriate is left unsaid or unclear, **we set youth up to fail.**

Youth are much more likely to rise to the challenge and engage in positive behaviors if boundaries are clearly stated up front and reinforced consistently.

Benefits for Youth Ministry

Fewer crises

Happier youth

Happier parents

Happier adult volunteers

More congregational support

Living the faith as a community

What's the Word?

Setting Boundaries Is Very Biblical!

God established a **covenant** with Abraham and his descendants.

You will be my people
 and I will be your God.

God gave the Law (boundaries) to help the people live in community with one another and more especially to live in faithful relationship to God.

The Law, included in Torah (the first five books of the Scriptures), set the Hebrew people apart as a covenant community. God's people were

blessed to be a blessing—

a shining light to the other nations.

The Ten Commandments set boundaries for the covenant community.

Jesus came to fulfill the Law. Through his life, teachings, death, and resurrection, we discover the essence of the Law—
love!

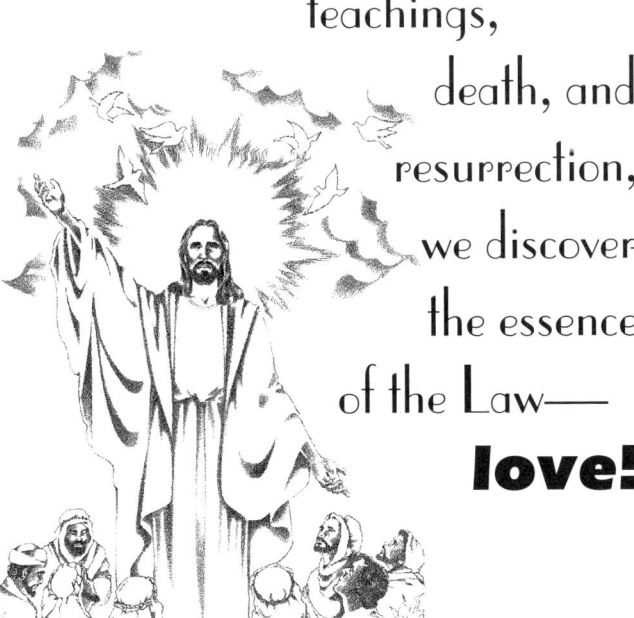

What's the Word?

The commandments, "You shall not commit adultery; You shall not murder; You shall not steal; You shall not covet;" and any other commandment are summed up in this word, "**Love** your neighbor as yourself." Love does no wrong to a neighbor; therefore, love is the fulfilling of the law.

—Romans 13:9-10

Remind them to be subject to rulers and authorities, to be obedient, to be ready for every good work, to speak evil of no one, to avoid quarreling, to be gentle, and to show courtesy to everyone.

—Titus 3:1-2

Both Old and New Testaments are filled with instructions for **proper religious and moral behavior.**

From the Ten Commandments to Jesus' teachings in Matthew 5 and 6 about living the spirit of the Law ("You have heard that it was said, ... but I say to you ..."), biblical authors explain and re-explain how to live a faith-filled, righteous life according to God's instructions.

Check out these passages for some more how-to's:

Galatians 5:13-26— Fruit of the Spirit

Colossians 3—Rules for Holy Living

2 Peter 1:5-8— What to Add to Faith

Scripture is also clear about how to handle **broken** boundaries...

John 8:1-11—The Woman Caught in Adultery

Galatians 6:1-10—Bear One Another's Burdens

1 Thessalonians 5:12-24—Admonish, Encourage, Be Patient

What's the Word?

What's the Word?

... as well as about our **attitude** when confronting broken boundaries.

Matthew 6:14-15—Forgive Others

Matthew 7:1-5—Do Not Judge

1 Peter 5:1-5—Clothe Yourself With Humility

Setting Boundaries—Creating Covenant

Why?

Boundaries help **minimize** discipline problems.

They also help **maximize** the potential for growth—on many levels.

For example, as youth help set and live within boundaries, they experience living in covenant. They gain a context for greater understanding of the Bible and the covenant relationship between God and God's people—including themselves.

When?

The most effective time to set boundaries with your youth is **at the beginning of the year or the first session** of your planned meetings. It is also helpful to revisit the group's boundaries

after a holiday or vacation break—
to refresh memories and commitments

before an upcoming event or trip—
to highlight specific boundaries

after a problem has occurred—
to remind everyone of the boundaries and why we follow them

What?

6 Prime Areas for Boundaries

Participation

Safety concerns

Property use

Legal issues

Language

Relationships, especially boy/girl

Setting Boundaries—Creating Covenant

Who?

An Advisory Group

Invite the leaders, pastor, parents, and other adults from your community to give specific input as to what behaviors are expected and appropriate for both youth and the adults who work with youth. Along with clarifying what is expected, these adults can also establish guidelines for what to do when boundaries are broken. (See more about consequences on pages 48–55.)

It will also be helpful to include selected youth in this initial conversation. These youth can provide insights and situational examples that can help determine clear, fair, and necessary guidelines for behavior.

The Youth

It is extremely important to involve the youth themselves in setting boundaries and expectations. Making youth a part of this process gives them an investment in the results. Also, the youth know best what some of the problem behaviors are, and they may shed some light on areas adults might not have realized needed addressing.

Setting Boundaries

How?

Ask the youth to make two lists in response to these two questions:

—What damages or destroys relationships?

—What builds or nurtures relationships?

Encourage the youth to name specific actions and attitudes that fit into each list.

Advise adults to wait to add to the lists until youth have finished. Adults will likely discover that the youth name some of the same issues and boundaries that the advisory group identified.

Setting Boundaries With Youth

Builds Relationships

Respect
Spending time together
Listening when someone speaks
Doing things as a team
Expressing appreciation

Damages Relationships

Rumors
Cheating
Names that put people down
Being two-faced
Talking behind someone's back

After completing the lists, ask

—What do you notice about these lists?

Again, allow plenty of time for their responses. If need be, point out that the contents of the lists

—usually are opposites of each other
—specifically express how people want or don't want to be treated
—often fall under one of the Ten Commandments

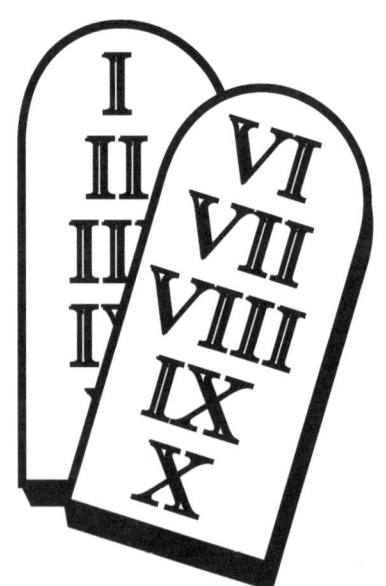

Refocus the group on the **goals** of the discussion:

—**To create an environment where people feel physically and emotionally safe.**
—**To have a group that builds and nourishes relationships.**
—**To create the kind of community we say we value as Christians.**

Ask the youth to condense the lists into the most important ones for the group. Have them name no more than ten. Create a new list that everyone agrees to and post it in the meeting space.

Our Top Ten Rules We Live By

1.
2.
3.
4.
5.
6.
7.
8.
9.
10.

Setting Boundaries—Creating Covenant

A Sample List

- Respect for all
- Participation
- Openness
- Attendance at whole program
- Phone use
  — Only before or after the program or in an emergency
- Restrooms
  — If you gotta' go, you gotta' go

Helpful Hints for Naming a Boundary

1. Keep it simple.
State the boundary clearly and concisely. "One person speaks at a time." "Disagree appropriately."

2. State it positively.
Tell what persons should do and how to do it. "Thou shall..." instead of "Thou shall not..." "Be in the gym at 7:45" instead of "Don't be late."

3. Stick to the Golden Rule (Luke 6:31).
Keep in mind how you want and deserve to be treated as a child of God.

Setting Boundaries—Creating Covenant

Sample Covenant for an Event

As representatives of Christ and his church, we, the participants in [event], take seriously our responsibility to care for one another. This covenant represents our affirmation of our concern for the well-being of the total community. We covenant with one another to insure the safety of all, to make our time together more meaningful, and to care for the space we share. We also agree specifically to

—leave vehicles parked and unoccupied
—remain on the site unless given permission to leave
—attend all activities, including meals
—never enter the room of someone of the other gender
—never use or bring alcohol, tobacco, or other illegal or dangerous materials
—respect the person and property of others

This covenant is made between each person and the whole group. In the case of a broken covenant, the group will be represented by the Covenant Advisory Team. I understand that if I break the covenant, and if the brokenness cannot be reconciled, I may be sent home at my own expense.

Signed,

—From *YouthNet* (Volume 4, Number 1), page 5

Communicate, Communicate!

After establishing boundaries (and appropriate consequences for breaking them), be sure everyone knows what they are. Communicate them to parents, any adults working with the youth, and of course, to the youth themselves.

Make sure that everyone knows that

1. There are specific boundaries for behaviors that everyone is expected to follow.
2. Maintaining these boundaries will help make this meeting time a safe and welcoming place.
3. There are preestablished and appropriate consequences for breaking boundaries.
4. Any broken boundaries will be addressed in a fair and dignified way. (More on this later.)

Setting Boundaries—Creating Covenant

MAINTAINING BOUNDARIES

2 Tried-and-True Tactics

1 PREVENTIVE TEACHING*

Set youth up for success.

Specifically name and briefly explain the boundaries and expected behaviors before each event or activity. A little Preventive Teaching goes a long way in stopping negative behaviors before they get started.

---

* Preventive Teaching and Effective Praise have been developed and are practiced consistently and successfully by the Youth Care Specialists of Boys Town.

SUCCESS

The Steps to Preventive Teaching

1. Describe the behaviors that are expected.

2. Give a reason.

3. Practice (optional).

Maintaining Boundaries

Preventive Teaching in Action

One thing I've learned from working with youth is that gossiping and complaining can quickly ruin a good session. Here's how I use Preventive Teaching before our discussions:

1. "When discussing a problem or situation, please do not use any names. Stick to talking only about yourself and your feelings. No blaming or complaining."

2. "It's important to do this for many reasons:
    —No one wants to be talked about behind his or her back.
    —It is not fair to discuss someone who is not present to speak to the issue.
    —We are about solving problems, not laying blame or complaining."

It's amazing how these simple boundaries have prevented potentially serious problems. They have also enabled the youth to speak more freely, trust one another more, and resolve conflicts in a more responsible fashion!

2 EFFECTIVE PRAISE

One of the best ways to help kids do the right thing is to **catch them being good!**

We all need reassurance that we're doing what we are supposed to. We all like to receive praise and compliments. A great way to ensure that a positive behavior is repeated is to praise it specifically.

Tell kids what they're doing right—**when they're doing it!**

Be sure to name what it is they are doing that has won your approval. Then they know exactly what to do right next time!

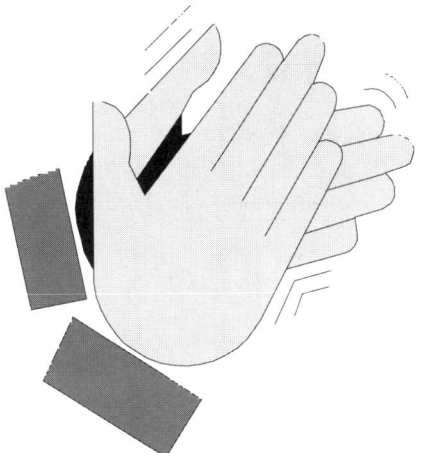

Maintaining Boundaries

The Steps to Effective Praise

1. Show your approval.
Smile, speak a word of praise or thanks, or give a pat on the back.

2. Describe the positive.
Name it specifically.

—"Tracy, thanks for waiting for Alberto to finish speaking before stating your point."
—"Peter, I really appreciated your call to let me know that you'd be late for the planning meeting."

3. Give a reason.
Tell them why what they did was good, important, or helpful.

—To Tracy: "Waiting for someone to finish speaking before you speak is a great way to show respect. It also shows that you are really listening."
—To Peter: "Your call helped me use that extra time wisely instead of worrying and waiting."

When a Boundary Is Broken

Consequences and Grace

Boundary breaking is **bound** to happen.

We all cross a boundary every now and then, sometimes by accident and sometimes on purpose. Some infractions are minor; others are major.

Our task as adults is to provide consistent management of boundaries, whether kept or broken. It's important to know in advance what to do when boundaries or rules are broken. Corrective Teaching, another tried-and-true method from the Youth Care Specialists at Boys Town, coupled with appropriate consequences, is a most effective method for turning a broken boundary into a **teachable moment** and possibly an **experience of grace.**

Corrective Teaching Steps

1 STOP THE PROBLEM BEHAVIOR

As soon as you notice a boundary broken, address it.

Sometimes just moving closer to the problem behavior, (moving to sit next to the two whispering teens), or catching the eye of those involved can stop the problem. Other times, a simple referral to the covenant, spoken in a calm and descriptive manner, can help persons get back on track. "Remember, no talking during the prayer service."

2 GIVE A CONSEQUENCE

Sometimes it is enough of a consequence to have an adult leader sit next to you or to be reminded of the covenant. Other times, a more substantial consequence may be needed.

BROKEN BOUNDARY: Aaron brings a six-pack of beer to the retreat.

CONSEQUENCES
- Confiscate the alcohol.
- As the leader, confront his behavior in private or with a small, designated Covenant Advisory Team that includes other youth.
- Notify his parents; take him home or have the parents do so.
- Work with Aaron to decide an appropriate expression to the group (an apology or restitution).
- Follow up with the parents so that you are working together to support Aaron in better behavior.

3 DESCRIBE THE POSITIVE BEHAVIOR HE OR SHE SHOULD DO

Now that the person knows what not to do, let him or her know what to do.

Whisper to Shannon, "Please give your quiet attention to our guest speaker."

4 GIVE YOUTH A CHANCE TO ENGAGE IN POSITIVE BEHAVIOR

Now back away; allow the youth to turn their own behavior around. Watch for any steps in the right direction and praise them for it.

Most often you can do Corrective Teaching calm, low voice-tones, one on one, without disturbing the rest of the group or calling the group's attention to the person. Of course, there may be times when you have to stop the group activity and address a major boundary breaking.

7 Guidelines for Consequences

1 DECIDE BEFOREHAND

Consequences should be established and communicated in advance. Don't wait for a situation to arise before deciding what the consequence will be. It is better to have predetermined consequences that are agreed upon by all the adults and well communicated to the teens.

Consequences decided on the spur of the moment can easily become too punishing.

2 GO FOR THE 3 R'S

Sometimes situations arise that no one thought about in advance. Consider using a Covenant Advisory Team, a few designated youth and adults who will seek resolution when a problem arises. Key questions the team needs to deal with are

—Who or what was injured?
—Where there justifying or mitigating circumstances?
—What resolution would build up the parties involved?
—What restitution does justice require? (Repair damages? Pay for broken property? Apologize? Do assigned tasks as a sign of remorse or repentance?)
—What would it take to restore the covenant?
—What follow up would be appropriate?

Resolution

Restitution

Restoration

—Terry Carty, "When the Covenant Is Broken," *YouthNet* (Volume 4, Number 1); page 1)

When a Boundary Is Broken

3 SEEK JUSTICE AND FORGIVENESS

Consequences should never be degrading or humiliating. They should be opportunities for learning responsibility and experiencing Christian love.

"Do not sacrifice forgiveness in the attempt to seek justice. Do not sacrifice justice in the attempt to reach forgiveness. Seek both accountability and grace."

—Terry Carty, "When the Covenant Is Broken," *YouthNet* (Volume 4, Number 1); page 1

4 APPLY TO ALL

Consequences should be given fairly and consistently. All youth should be held accountable for maintaining these boundaries. Don't play favorites or let some talk their way out of owning up to their behaviors.

5 PRAISE IN PUBLIC— CORRECT IN PRIVATE

Corrective teaching and consequences should be done one-to-one whenever possible, even if it means taking a youth aside for a moment. Except in minor cases, it is rarely effective to correct a youth in front of a group. Usually this approach causes anger and embarrassment, and you run the risk of escalating the problem rather than correcting it.

6 GET HELP

Ask for help from parents and other adults. Sometimes the mere presence of more adults help youth stay on track.

The Fireside Option
At Calvary Church, all youth know that if they are struggling to maintain decent behavior in youth group, they will be asked to join the parents in the Fireside Area and just hang with them for a while.

The parents don't point fingers or lecture. However, they provide the teens space to collect themselves again to reenter group life with appropriate behavior. The Fireside Option frees the adults leading youth group from worry about discipline problems.

7 MOVE ON

Once the incident is over, don't bring it up again!

Addressing and correcting any problems promptly and without much disruption sends a powerful message to the whole group. It lets them know that

—you are **watching** out for them,
—you **care** about how they treat one another, and
—you **keep** your word.

They need to see that you will be firm, yet gentle, in safeguarding their boundaries. Your actions speak much louder than words in these instances.

Broken Boundaries

The Golden Rule of Consequences

Remember the Golden Rule (Luke 6:31) when correcting behaviors:

"Do to others as you would have them do to you."

Put yourself in that teen's place.

Broken Boundaries

Treat young persons the way you want to be treated—

the way

JESUS

would treat them.

When a Boundary Is Broken

Broken Boundaries

Show genuine empathy and understanding rather than anger or dominance. When dealing with difficult situations, remember these two adages:

"**Love** the sinner, hate the sin!"

"A soft answer turns away wrath, but a harsh word stirs up anger." —Proverbs 15:1

Pontius' Puddle

When a Boundary Is Broken

Basic Boundaries

10 Boundaries for Discussions Everyone Can Feel Good About

1. **One person speaks at a time.**

2. **Disagree without being disagreeable**

3. **No put downs.**
   Show respect to others by refraining from making value judgments about them. You may not use words like stupid, dumb, ugly, gross, or other judgmental or negative words to describe people or their thoughts. Say "Please be quiet" instead of "Shut up!" No teasing, even if only in fun.

4. **Say whatever you want (as long as it is on the topic and without using obscene or offensive language).**

5. **What is said here, stays here.**
   The exception is when an adult needs to seek help for a teen in danger.

6. **Self-disclose appropriately—no personal dumping, public confessions, blaming, or complaining.**

7. **Practice good listening skills: Look at the person who is speaking; concentrate on what is being said, and so forth.**

8. **Ask for clarification whenever you need it.**

9. **Laugh with people not at them.**

10. **Participate!**
    You'll get out of the discussion what you put into it. So get into it!

Boundaries For One-to-Ones

3 Crucial Rules for Youth-Adult Interactions

When a teen asks to talk to you privately, there are some important boundaries to observe and to make known.

1 SOME THINGS YOU CANNOT KEEP CONFIDENTIAL

Let teens know that if they talk about thoughts of hurting themselves or someone else or if they reveal involvement in illegal, sexual, or abusive activity, you have a moral (and in some cases, legal) obligation to tell someone else who can help them. In these serious circumstances a teen's physical and/or emotional life is at stake. We must let youth know that we value their life above all else, even above their possible anger at "telling on" them.

2 MEET IN AN OPEN SPACE WHERE YOU CAN BE SEEN, BUT NOT OVERHEARD, BY OTHERS.

If meeting in an office, keep the door open or use an office with uncovered windows. Turn on a small fan to create just enough "white noise" to keep your conversation private. These precautions can prevent any allegations of misconduct and provide both of you with the security of knowing that others are around.

Boundaries for One-to-Ones

3 BE PREPARED TO MAKE REFERRALS.

If you are not a trained counselor, be careful not to overstep your bounds. Your appropriate role will be to point youth in the right direction and support them in getting the help they need if the problem is beyond your scope of expertise.

Have referral sources available with names and phones numbers of professionals who can help.

For Kids and Parents:
If you or someone you know
has a problem or is trouble,
call the Boys Town National Hotline.

Call toll-free, anytime.

PREVENTING PROBLEMS

Boundary Setting Skills for Youth

The best way to resolve a problem is to prevent it!

Teaching and modeling good boundary setting skills in youth groups can help prevent conflict and other problems. Learning more about and practicing social skills can help youth relate to one another and to adults in a more appropriate and Christian fashion.

Have youth roleplay situations and use the following skills. The practice will pay off.

The following skills are from *Teaching Social Skills to Youth*, by Tom Dowd and Jeff Tierney (Boys Town Press, 1992). Used with permission.

Saying No Assertively

- Look at the person.
- Use a clear, firm voice tone.
  - Say, "No, I don't want..."
- Request that the person leave you alone.
- Remain calm but serious.
- If possible, remove yourself from the situation.

Accepting No Answers

- Look at the person.
- Try to relax and stay calm.
- Listen carefully.

- Say, "OK."
- Take a deep breath if you feel upset.
- Don't sound angry or start to argue.

- Calmly ask a reason if you really don't understand.
- If you ask calmly, people will recognize you are serious about wanting to know a reason.
- Don't keep asking for reasons after you receive one.

- If you disagree, bring it up later.
- If you disagree right away, you will appear to be arguing.
- Plan what you are going to say.
- Be sure to thank the person for listening.

Responding to Teasing

- Remain calm, but serious.
- Assertively ask the person to stop teasing.
- If the teasing doesn't stop, ignore the other person or remove yourself.
- If the teasing stops, thank the other person for stopping and explain how teasing makes you feel.
- Report continued teasing or hazing to an adult.

Mini-Workshop

For Leaders

minutes

WELCOME/INTRODUCTIONS   5–10
Opening Prayer and Scripture Reading—Colossians 3:12-17

WHAT'S OUR IDEAL CHRISTIAN TEEN?   10–12
Together brainstorm what the ideal Christian teen would be like—how he or she would act, talk, treat others, spend free time, and so forth. List the responses. Refer to the list as appropriate throughout the workshop.

	minutes

WHAT ARE BOUNDARIES? (pages 4–15)   8–10
Either together or in two small groups create a two lists:
Examples of Boundaries and Benefits of Boundaries.

WHAT'S THE WORD? (pages 16–24)   10–20
Explain the concept of covenant. Assign small groups or pairs to review and report on the Scripture passages on their assigned page (page 22, 23, or 24).

SETTING BOUNDARIES—CREATING COVENANT   10–15
(pages 25–37)
Discuss the techniques. Address any questions.

PRACTICE BREAK (pages 38–42)   10–20
Create some scenarios and roleplay Preventive Teaching and Effective Praise.

minutes

SETTING CONSEQUENCES—LEAVING ROOM FOR GRACE (pages 43–57)   10–20

Talk about preferred ways of handling situations when a boundary is broken. Inform the group of any congregational policies.

PRACTICE BREAK (pages 43–57)   10–20

Create some scenarios and roleplay Corrective Teaching and dealing with consequences with grace.

PREVENTING PROBLEMS (pages 58–59, 63–66)   10–15

Discuss the need for teaching youth these basic skills. Practice the steps.

	minutes

BOUNDARIES FOR ADULTS (pages 60–62) — 8–10
Review the what's and why's. Give out appropriate local referral numbers.

RETURN TO THE WORD — 5–8
Have group reread Colossians 3:12-17; ask how Paul's instructions and our description of the ideal teen are similar? different? Affirm the role of positive discipline in achieving the ideal.

CLOSING — 2–3
Pray for each young person and for the opportunities for grace and growth that lie ahead.

THE BIG PICTURE

Working with youth is a little like putting together a jigsaw puzzle: It helps to have a picture of what it's supposed to look like! (See page 73.)

In effective youth ministry **vision** is central.

Seven major elements contribute to realizing that vision. The more of them that are developed and in place, the better.

Youth ministry planners in individual churches can develop each of those areas **their own way**, according to their congregation's particular resources, gifts, and priorities and the needs of their youth.

The Big Picture

The Big Picture

How does this SkillAbility fit in this big picture? Here are just a few of the ways. By using ideas in this book, not only do you create a safe and welcoming place for young persons to grow in their relationship with God and others, you also

- create an **ETHOS** of respect for one another that builds relationships among youth and gives the group a distinctive identity as Christian

- give youth **EXPERIENCES** in learning the Word and living the faith through their being a part of a grace-filled, covenant relationship

- foster skills for youth going into the **COMMUNITY** as credible witnesses for the faith

YOUTH MINISTRY: A COMPREHENSIVE APPROACH

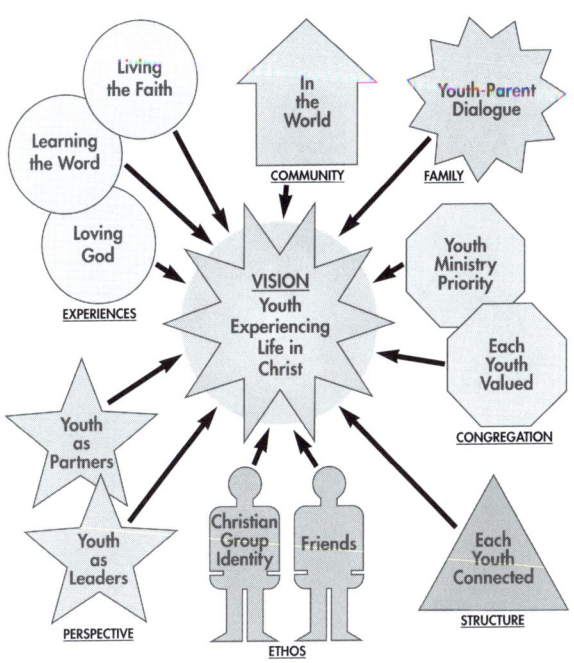

The Big Picture

FAMILY

The Big Picture

Research is clear that **parent-youth dialogue** about matters of faith is crucial for youth to develop mature faith. Youth themselves express desire to be listened to, to have boundaries, and to have parental involvement in their lives. Parents need skills for relating to their changing teens as well as assurance that their values and voice do matter to their youth. How do we in the church facilitate parent-youth dialogue?

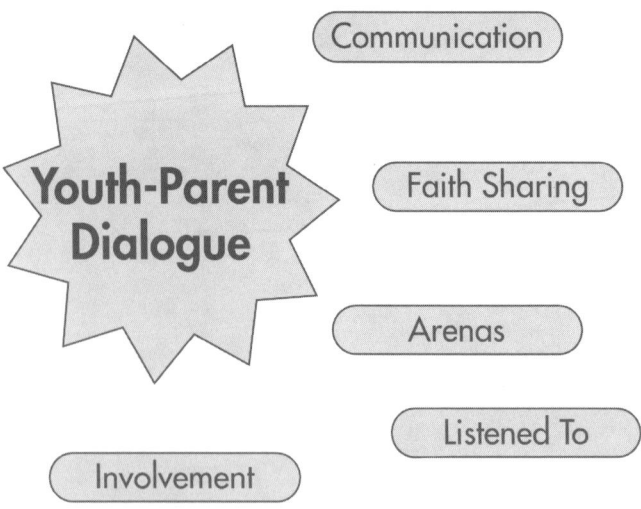

CONGREGATION

Youth ministry is the ministry of the whole congregation, beginning with making **youth ministry a priority**: prayer for the ministry, people (not just one person), time, effort, training, resources, and funding. The goal for the congregation is **each youth valued**. Interaction with adults, including mentors, positive language about youth, prayer partners for each one, simply being paid attention to—these are active roles for the congregation.

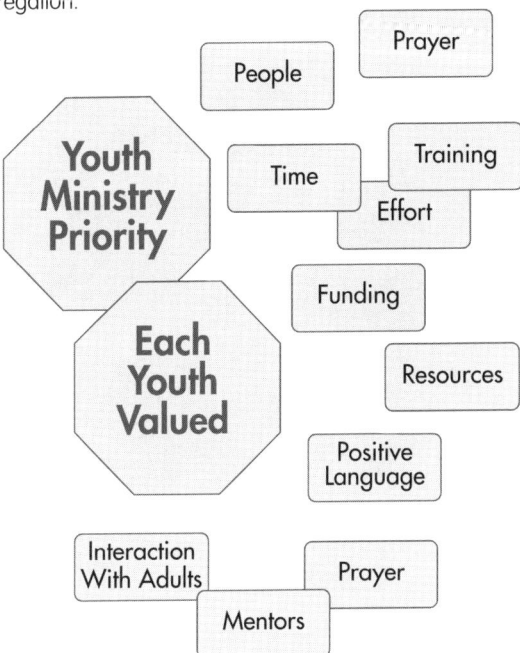

The Big Picture

STRUCTURE

Whatever shape the ministry takes, the goal is to have **each youth connected**. Sunday school and youth group are only a beginning. What are the needs of the youth? What groups (even of only 2 or 3 youth) and what times would help connect young people to the faith community? How easy is it for new youth to enter? How well do we stay in touch with the changing needs of our youth? Do we have structures in place that facilitate communication? outreach? "How" can vary; it's the "why" that's crucial.

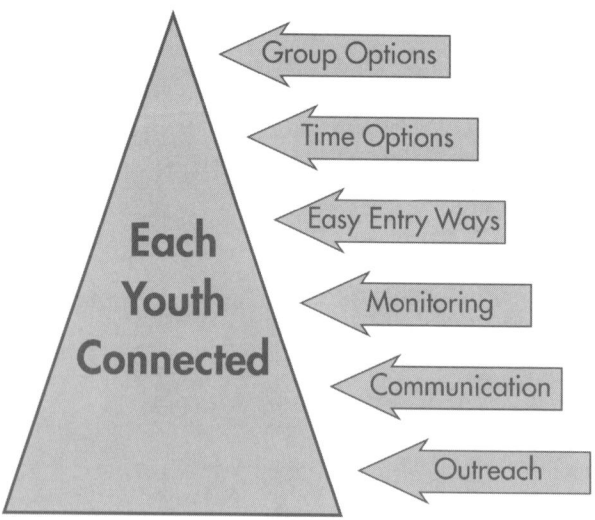

ETHOS

We are relational beings; we all need **friends**. The support, caring, and accountability friends provide help youth experience the love of God. As those friendships are nurtured within **Christian group identity**, young people claim for themselves a personal identity of being Christian. What language, rituals, traditions, and bonding experiences mark each grouping within the youth ministry as distinctively Christian?

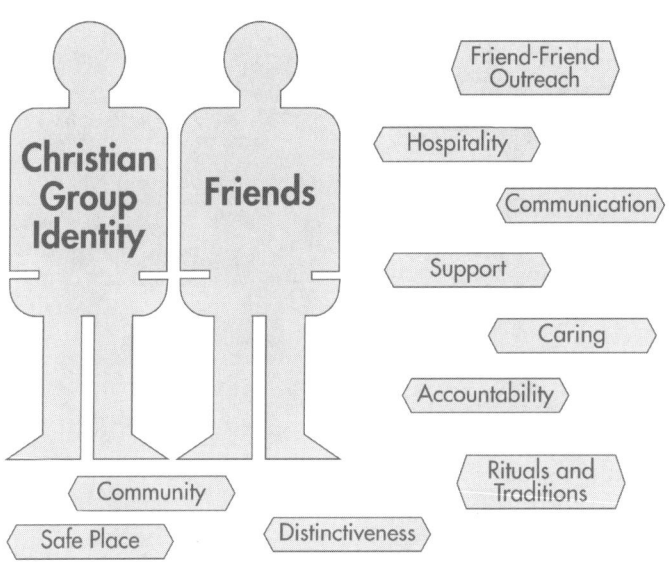

The Big Picture

The Big Picture

PERSPECTIVE

Youth are keenly aware of being seen as problems, being treated as objects to be fixed, or as recipients too inexperienced to have anything to offer. What would happen if we operated from the perspective of seeing **youth as leaders, youth as partners**? We would listen to them more, be intentional about identifying their gifts, take seriously their input, encourage their decision making, and train them for leadership roles.

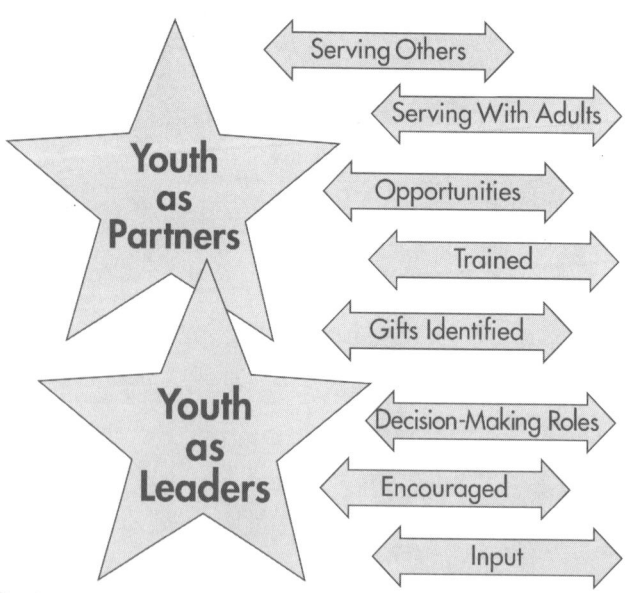

Setting Boundaries With Youth

EXPERIENCES

Worship, devotions, prayer, and participation in the community of faith build for youth the experience of **loving God**. Study and reflection upon the Bible and the faith are crucial for **learning the Word**. Being among people who are Christian role models and grappling with difficult moral, ethical, justice, and stewardship issues help young people with **living the faith**. Curriculum resources specifically provide material to facilitate these three kinds of experiences.

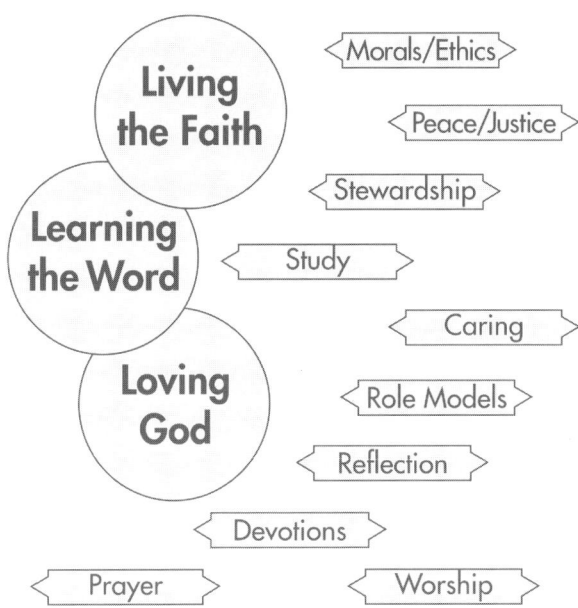

The Big Picture

COMMUNITY

As Christians, youth are challenged to be **in the world** as servants, as witnesses, as leaven—making a difference with their lives, giving others a glimpse of the Kingdom. What opportunities, what training, what support do we give youth to equip them for ministry beyond the walls of the church building?

In the World

Serving

Witnessing

Leaven/Salt/Light